W9-ATQ-958

12-28-04

(26)   2 copies

The Shepherd's Story

Published in Nashville, Tennessee, by Oliver-Nelson Books, a division of Thomas Nelson, Inc., Publishers, and distributed in Canada by Lawson Falle, Ltd., Cambridge, Ontario.

ISBN 0-8407-3415-8

Manufactured in Singapore.

1 2 3 4 5 6 7 — 97 96 95 94 93 92

The Shepherd's Story

Halcyon Backhouse

Illustrated by
Annabel Spenceley

A Division of Thomas Nelson Publishers
Nashville

I will not forget that night.
We had lit a fire
to keep our sheep safe.
Wolves are scared of fire.
Soon we were scared, too,
but not of the fire.

We sat and we talked.
Then we saw a bright light.
And in the light was an angel!
I went hot and cold.
I felt sick.
Then the angel spoke.

"Do not be scared," he said.
His voice was like music.
"I have good news.
Your King has been born.
You will find Him
in King David's town.
He is in a manger."
"What!" I said.
"He is where animals eat?"

Then the sky was full of angels.
Lots of them.
And they were singing.
"Glory to God," they said.
"And peace on earth to those
God is pleased with."

Then the angels went away.
And there were just us
and the sheep.
I said, "Let us go to town.
Let us see what God has
told us about."

The town was crowded.
"Let us try the inn," I said.
"Try the stable," someone said.
"The stable!" I said.
"What sort of place is that
for a baby King?"

But there He was,
just like the angel had said.
He was asleep.
We stood outside.
We did not go in.
It did not seem right.

"Come on in,"
His mother said.
She smiled at us.
And we all began to talk
at the same time.

After that we told
the story to everyone
we met.
Some people said
we were crazy.
But we did not care.
"Praise God!" we kept saying.
"God is great."

Then we went back to the sheep.
God had kept them safe.
Now I think about that angel
and the baby.
The King has come!
Hurrah!
I cannot wait till He grows up.